FRANCE

WORLD ADVENTURES

BY STEFFI CAVELL-CLARKE

BookLife

©2018
Book Life
King's Lynn
Norfolk PE30 4LS

ISBN: 978-1-78637-264-2

Written by:
Steffi Cavell-Clarke

Edited by:
Kirsty Holmes

Designed by:
Dan Scase

A catalogue record for this book
is available from the British Library.

FRANCE
WORLD ADVENTURES

CONTENTS

Words in **red** can be found in the glossary on page 24.

3

WHERE IS FRANCE?

France is a country found on the **continent** of Europe. It is one of the biggest European countries.

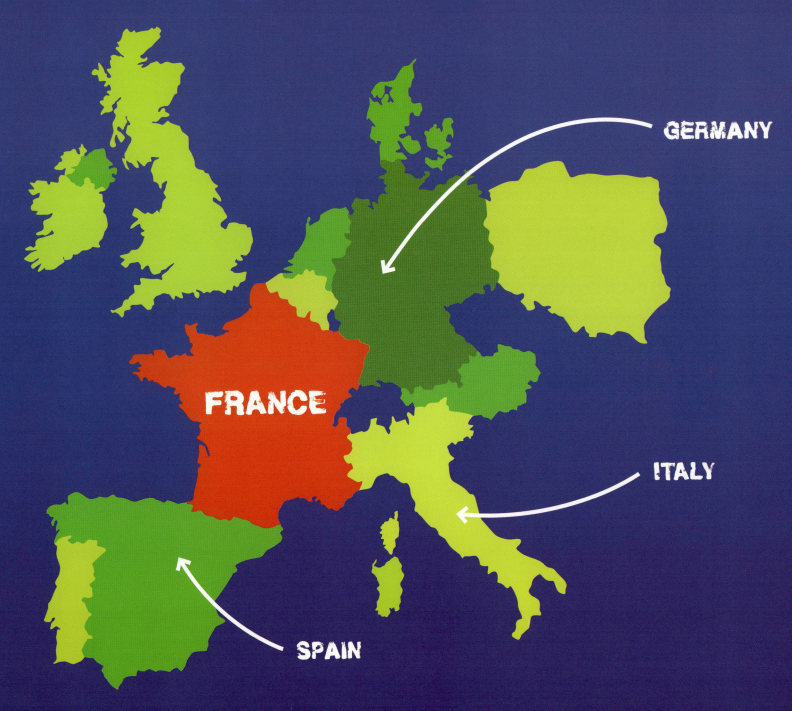

GERMANY

FRANCE

ITALY

SPAIN

The **population** of France is over 66 million. Millions of people live in big cities, such as Paris or Marseille.

PARIS, FRANCE

WEATHER AND LANDSCAPE

The weather in France changes with the seasons. It has hot, dry summers and cool, wet winters. The hottest months of the year are usually July, August and September.

The landscape in France changes from place to place. There are big cities, small farms, green forests and high mountains.

There are also lots of **vineyards** in France where grapes are grown.

CLOTHING

French people mostly wear **modern** clothing, such as jeans and T-shirts. Some people wear a traditional French hat called a beret.

BERET

BONNET

BLOUSE

SKIRT

For **festivals** and parties, people still dress up in **traditional** French clothes. Women wear white blouses, bonnets and long skirts.

RELIGION

There are many different **religions** that people follow. The religion with the most followers in France is Christianity. Most Christians in France are **Roman Catholic**.

The Roman Catholic place of **worship** is a church.
Many Catholics visit the church every Sunday for prayer.

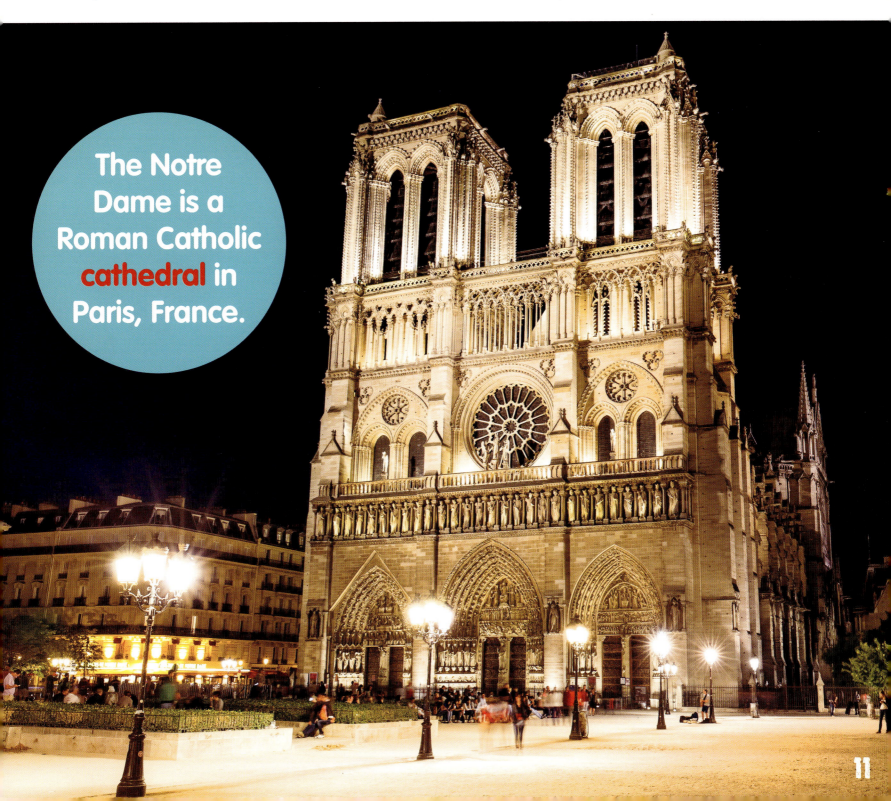

The Notre Dame is a Roman Catholic **cathedral** in Paris, France.

BAGUETTE

FOOD

France is known for making some of the best cheese, bread and wine in the world. Loaves of bread called baguettes are eaten with most meals.

There are many traditional French treats that are now eaten and enjoyed all around the world. Croissants and macarons are enjoyed in France and other countries.

CROISSANTS

MACARONS

AT SCHOOL

In France, children start school at 6 years old and study until they are 18 years old. Some French primary schools are closed on Wednesdays.

Children in France study French, English, maths, science and history. Most children go to school to study, but some children are taught at home.

AT HOME

Many people in France live in big cities. In cities, like Paris, most of the people live in flats. Some windows have wooden shutters to keep the rooms cool in the hot summers.

Lots of people in France also live in the countryside. Many famers grow olive trees there. The olives can be eaten or made into oil for cooking.

FAMILIES

Most children live with their parents, brothers and sisters. Some children live with other family members, like their grandparents.

In France, families often get together to celebrate Christian festivals such as Christmas and Easter.

SPORT

Fans supporting the French football team.

Sports, such as basketball, tennis, football and rugby are all very popular in France.

Lots of people in France enjoy cycling too.
Many people from other countries visit France to
ride their bikes through the beautiful landscapes.

France is home to the Tour de France, which is the world's most famous cycle race.

FUN FACTS

Millions of people visit Paris every year. They visit the Louvre, the Eiffel Tower, Notre Dame and the Arc de Triomphe.

THE LOUVRE

EIFFEL TOWER

ARC DE TRIOMPHE

NOTRE DAME

Mont Blanc is the highest mountain in France at 4,810 metres. The river Loire is the longest river with a length of 1,012 kilometres.

RIVER LOIRE

FRANCE

MONT BLANC

GLOSSARY

cathedral	a large building used for Christian worship
continent	very large areas of land that are made up of many countries
festivals	times when people come together to celebrate special events
modern	from recent or present times
population	the number of people living in a place
religions	systems of faith and worship
Roman Catholic	a member of the Roman Catholic church
traditional	related to very old behaviours or beliefs
vineyards	a piece of land where vines are grown
worship	a religious act where a person expresses their love for a god

INDEX

Photocredits: Abbreviations: l-left, r-right, b-bottom, t-top, c-centre, m-middle.

Front Cover – Syda Productions, bg – Aleksey Klints. 1 – Aleksey Klints. 2 – asife. 3 – Syda Productions. 5 – Luciano Mortula – LGM. 6 – MarinaDa. 7 – Gayane. 8 – racorn. 9 – Wikipedia. 10 – wavebreakmedia. 11 – maziarz. 12 – MasterQ. 13 – Ekaterina Markelova. 14 – DGLimages. 15 – Photographee.eu. 16 – WDG Photo. 17bg – visuall2. 17tr – Jacques PALUT. 18 – Carlos Horta. 19 – Pressmaster. 20 – Phovoir. 21 – ChiccoDodiFC. 22ml – NODIYA ILYA. 22mr – givaga. 22bl – TTstudio. 22br – RomanSlavik.com. 23bg – By Jakub Cejpek. 23tr – Ander Dylan. Images are courtesy of Shutterstock.com. With thanks to Getty Images, Thinkstock Photo and iStockphoto.